Origins

Building Wembley

Steve Parker

Contents

OXFORD

UNIVERSITY PRESS

The last match

It is October 2000. England is playing football against Germany at Wembley **Stadium** in London. The stadium is packed with fans.

FIFA 2002 WORLD CUP QUAL
TIME:91
ENGLAND 0
GERMANY 1

England's last match at the old Wembley Stadium was a **qualifying** game for the 2002 World Cup. The Final score was 1–0 to Germany.

Wembley has seen many big events but the stadium is now too old. The seats are cramped. Some seats are so far from the pitch, fans cannot see the action. There are queues for almost everything.

BUILDING WEMBLEY TIMELINE

2000
2001
2002
2003
2004
2005
2006
2007

It's time to build a new Wembley Stadium. A bigger, better one!

A new start

Plans for the new Wembley Stadium are just beginning. The planners have to decide what the stadium will look like.

The plans for the new stadium are discussed.

The plans for the new stadium are made on computers and big sheets of paper. Every part is included, from the huge roof arch to the door handles.

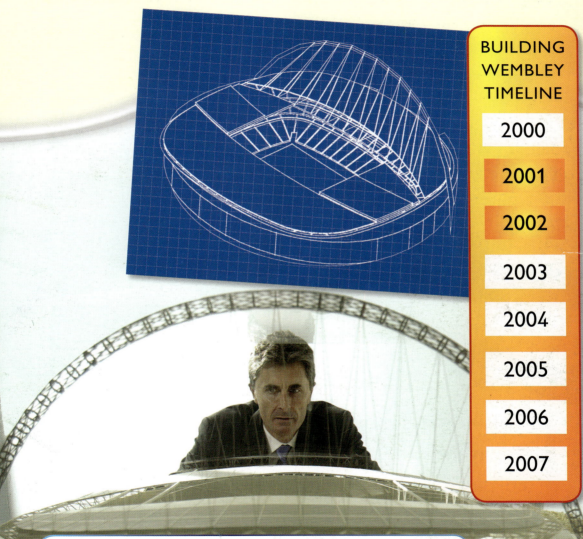

BUILDING WEMBLEY TIMELINE

2000

2001

2002

2003

2004

2005

2006

2007

People come to see a model of the new stadium. Everyone must agree that this is the best **design**.

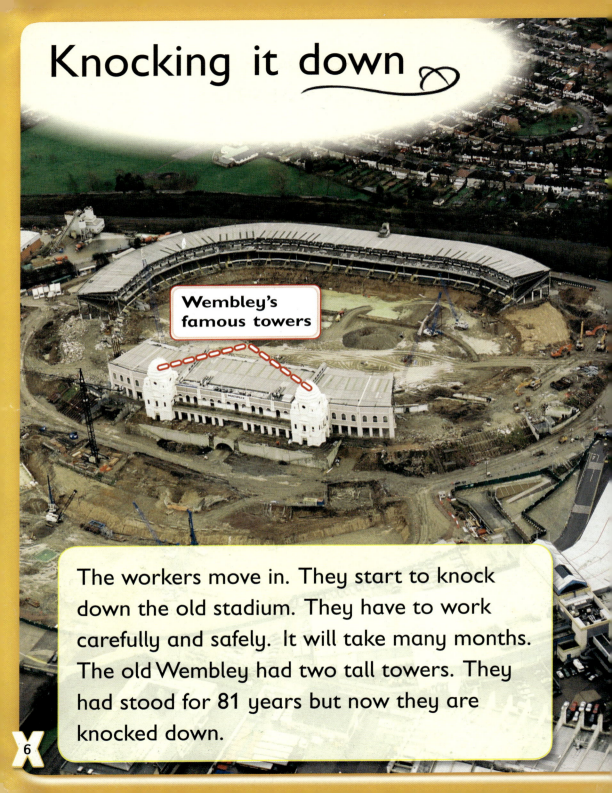

Knocking it down

Wembley's famous towers

The workers move in. They start to knock down the old stadium. They have to work carefully and safely. It will take many months. The old Wembley had two tall towers. They had stood for 81 years but now they are knocked down.

Now the site is clear, work on the new stadium can begin. Posts mark where the walls, towers and pitch will go.

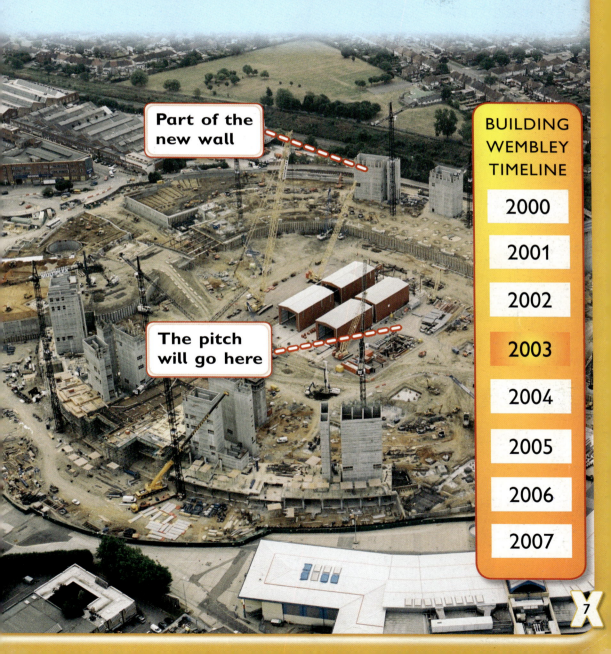

Part of the new wall

The pitch will go here

BUILDING WEMBLEY TIMELINE

2000

2001

2002

2003

2004

2005

2006

2007

Big holes

Work on the new stadium has started but it's going down, not up! First, lots of holes must be dug.

These huge holes will be the rooms and car parks.

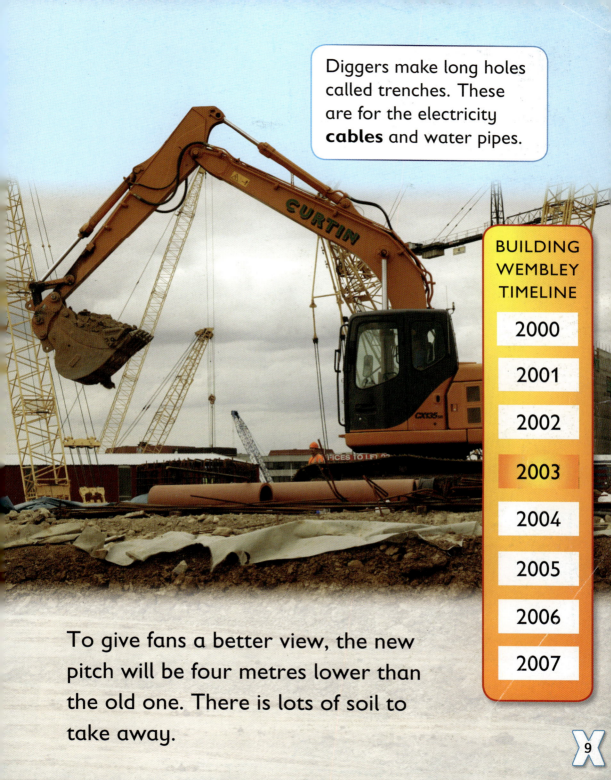

Diggers make long holes called trenches. These are for the electricity **cables** and water pipes.

BUILDING WEMBLEY TIMELINE

2000

2001

2002

2003

2004

2005

2006

2007

To give fans a better view, the new pitch will be four metres lower than the old one. There is lots of soil to take away.

Building starts

1 Trucks start to arrive with the building materials.

2 Huge drills make holes in the ground for rods (called piles).

3 Trucks pour concrete around the piles. The concrete hardens. This will be the strong **base** for the new stadium.

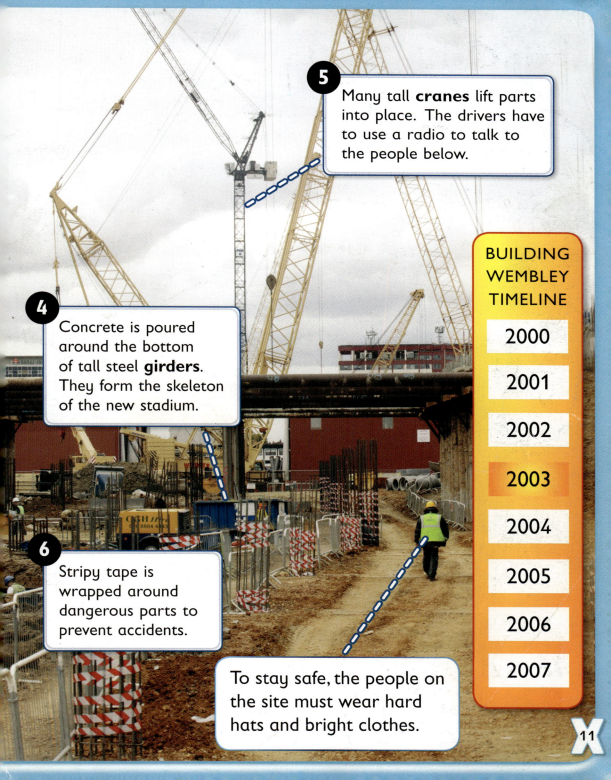

5 Many tall **cranes** lift parts into place. The drivers have to use a radio to talk to the people below.

4 Concrete is poured around the bottom of tall steel **girders**. They form the skeleton of the new stadium.

6 Stripy tape is wrapped around dangerous parts to prevent accidents.

To stay safe, the people on the site must wear hard hats and bright clothes.

BUILDING WEMBLEY TIMELINE

2000

2001

2002

2003

2004

2005

2006

2007

11

Taking shape

The stadium starts to take shape. The tall beams and strong girders will hold up the seats. The site is now very busy. There are more than 2000 workers.

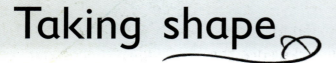

The girders are joined by heating them with a special flame. They get so hot that the metal melts and flows together. Then it cools and goes hard. This is called welding.

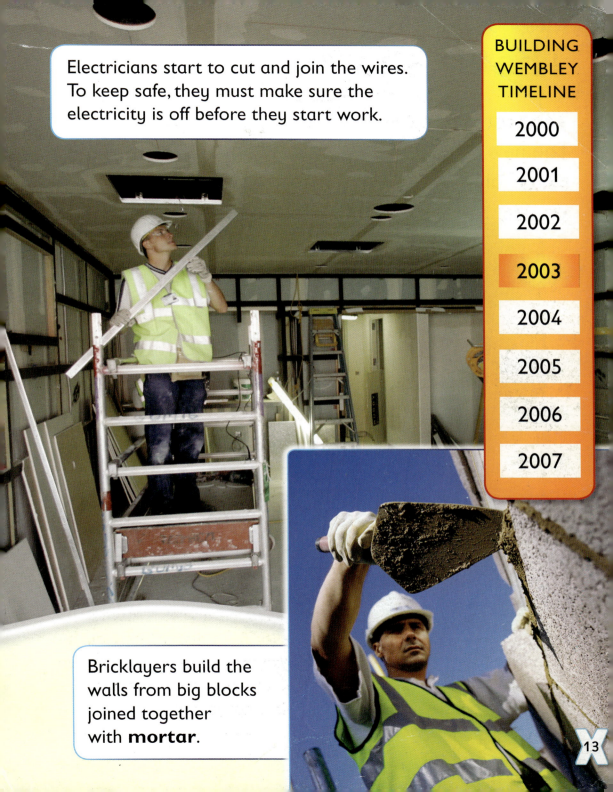

Electricians start to cut and join the wires. To keep safe, they must make sure the electricity is off before they start work.

BUILDING WEMBLEY TIMELINE

2000

2001

2002

2003

2004

2005

2006

2007

Bricklayers build the walls from big blocks joined together with **mortar**.

The Wembley arch

The two towers have been knocked down.
The new stadium will have a huge steel arch
that is higher than the towers.

The arch has 41 rings. They form a tunnel that is so big a train could pass through!

The parts of the arch are lifted by a huge crane and joined together.

BUILDING WEMBLEY TIMELINE

2000

2001

2002

2003

2004

2005

2006

2007

A sliding roof

The new Wembley Stadium will be like a giant bowl. There will be 90 000 seats under the huge roof. Everyone will have a great view!

Massive sloping girders are fixed in place to hold up the steps and seats.

The roof does not cover the pitch. The grass needs sunshine and rain to grow.

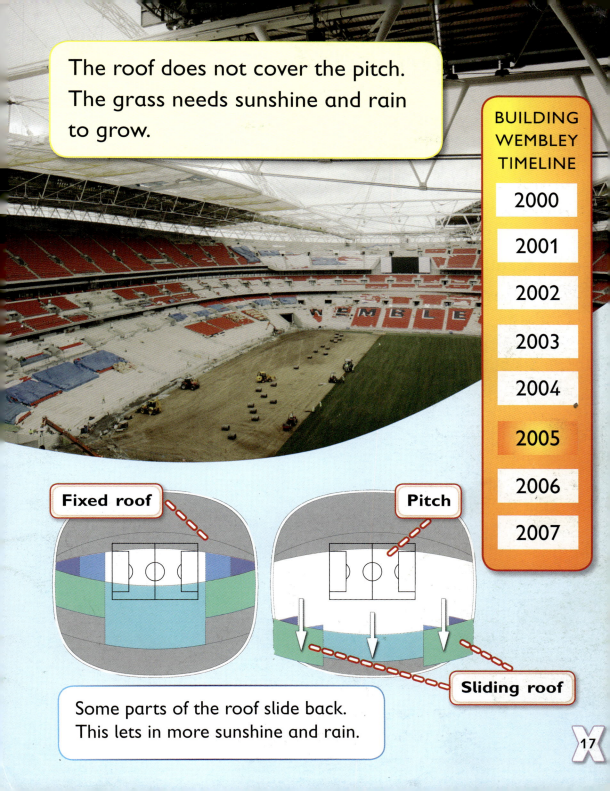

Fixed roof

Pitch

Sliding roof

Some parts of the roof slide back. This lets in more sunshine and rain.

17

Safe and secure

The new Wembley Stadium must be:
- comfortable
- safe
- easy to clean.

It must also save on resources like energy and water.

The seats have plenty of room for people's legs.

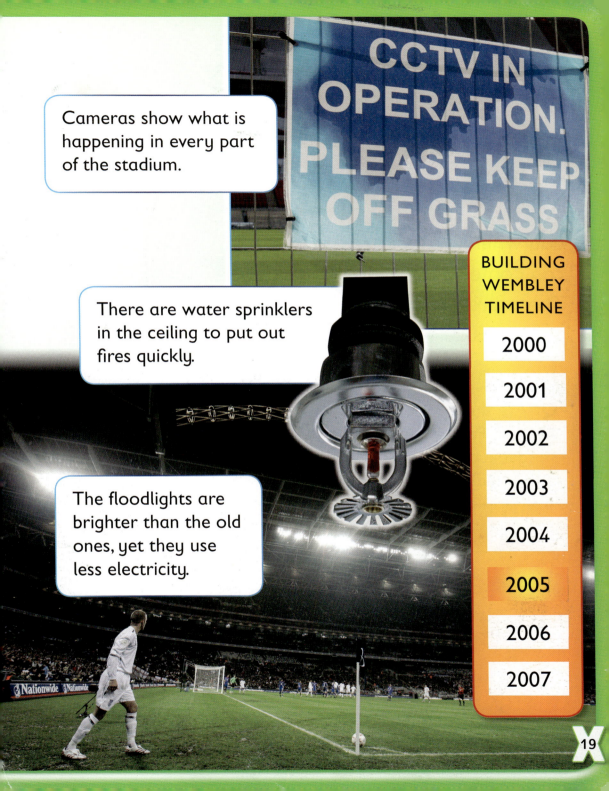

Cameras show what is happening in every part of the stadium.

CCTV IN OPERATION. PLEASE KEEP OFF GRASS

There are water sprinklers in the ceiling to put out fires quickly.

The floodlights are brighter than the old ones, yet they use less electricity.

BUILDING WEMBLEY TIMELINE

2000

2001

2002

2003

2004

2005

2006

2007

Nearly finished

The new stadium will soon be open. It is time to see how it works. There is a practice day when local people can come in for a look. These are the questions people ask:

Q: Are there enough ways in?
A: Yes! People must be able to get in and out quickly. There should be no long queues.

Alan Ball MBE
1966 World Cup Winner
1945-2007

Q: Can everyone see?
A: Yes! Two giant screens show replays, scores and other information. Each screen is as big as 600 televisions.

Q: Is there enough food?
A: Yes! Hungry fans all want to eat at half-time. The biggest kitchen is one-third the size of the football pitch!

Q: Are there enough toilets?
A: Yes! The new stadium has 2600 toilets. That is more than any other building in the world.

BUILDING WEMBLEY TIMELINE

2000

2001

2002

2003

2004

2005

2006

2007

Open at last

It has taken seven years to build the new Wembley Stadium. At last England's football team can play on their home pitch again.

The first England match is against the world champions, Brazil. The teams play hard and the score is 1–1.

The real winner of the day is the new Wembley Stadium. Everything works well. Everyone agrees the stadium is a great success.

Wembley Stadium is not just used for football matches. Rugby and other sports are played here too. It is also used by some of the biggest pop stars and bands in the world.

BUILDING WEMBLEY TIMELINE

2000

2001

2002

2003

2004

2005

2006

2007

London has a new **landmark**. The huge Wembley arch looks amazing at night. It is lit by more than 250 energy-saving lights!

Glossary

arch	a curved part of a building
base	the bottom part of something
cables	strong, thick wire or rope
crane	a machine for lifting heavy things
design	to draw a plan for something
girder	a large, long piece of metal
landmark	an important building or place
mortar	a mixture of sand and water, used to stick bricks together
pile	a long, thin piece of metal that is hammered into the ground, used to support a building
qualifying	you need to win your qualifying games to go through to the next round
recycle	to use things again instead of throwing them away
stadium	a large place where people can watch sport and games

Index